Deep Feelings
The Valley

THE DEEP FEELINGS SERIES
BOOK 2

Carlie Thrasher Downey

BREVIN, LLC

Published by:

Brevin, LLC
Scottsdale, Arizona

ISBN: 978-0-9853725-9-0

Cover and interior by Gary A. Rosenberg
Produced by The Book Couple • www.thebookcouple.com

Printed in the United States of America

*All Scripture quotations are taken from
the King James Version (K J V) of the Holy Bible!*

Contents

Acknowledgments

To the many people throughout the years,
Who have shared my laughter and my tears!

My Savior, Jesus Christ, for His sacrificial death and resurrection, so I could be born again; and for the gift of rhyme.

My parents: Carl C. (Bill) & Minnie B. Thrasher, for giving me birth and many cherished years of memories.

My teachers: Lemoine Young (Athens Jr. High School), for helping me to improve my self-esteem; and a special Sunday school teacher, Robbie Jordan, for taking me deeper into the Word of God.

My family: a daughter, Cathy & husband Randy Byers; and two sons, Darryl McGee & wife Valarie, and Terry McGee; Two granddaughters, Stacie & Tracie; and four great granddaughters, Randi, Kalee, Mackenzie, and Gracie; one niece, Sharon.

My mentor & confidants: Oleta Morton and Thelma Temple.

To my many friends, past and present who shared a part of themselves—from them came the birth of poetic inspiration!

Dedicated to the memory of:

E. J. McGee: my children's dad

Carl C. & Minnie B. Thrasher: my parents

Billie Thrasher Wood: my sister

*Cecil Downey: my husband, sweetheart,
and true soul mate*

Life is like a seesaw,
Today on top of the mountain,
Tomorrow in the deepest valley!

Introduction

I THANK GOD FOR JESUS, for my salvation, and for allowing me, by the Holy Spirit, to feel His presence as I read the Bible.

Sometimes a scripture sets a poem in motion, other times, as I'm writing a poem, a scripture comes alive and fits the poem. People, places, animals, or everyday happenings trigger my imagination. I feel so blessed that it was in God's plan to allow me such an enjoyable way of expressing my inner feelings.

Too Far—Too Fast—Too Soon

What Happened
To my childhood treasure;
I can not recall,
A memorable pleasure!
I received my last doll
When I was five,
Was no longer a child
By the age of seven,
Felt like and old woman
Time I was eleven!
Now I think my brain
Is more dead than alive!

Tracie, my granddaughter

Too Late I Learn

My storehouse of love
Wasn't filled to the top
And I was afraid to give it away.
I closed the door to my heart
'Cause I didn't know how to stop
Living in a dysfunctional way!

I vividly recall
Love came with a price
Much too high to pay!
I believed I must sacrifice
So I kept everyone at bay!

It's hard to teach another,
What wasn't taught to me
So the cycle goes unbroken;
Those hurting accusations
Linger in my memory,
For loving words were left unspoken!

Too late I learn
My children suffered from my mistakes,
For they needed attention and fun,
This makes my heart ache
'Cause I can't turn back time
Or undo what I've done!

The Gala Affair

As I walked from the mailbox
With an invitation in hand,
I eagerly read the word, AWARD,
At the M G M Grand!
Then I felt my heart skip a beat,
As my bare feet danced in the sand!

I thought, this must be a dream,
With this honor you wish to bestow!
Then the dream quickly vanished
Like teardrops in fluffy white snow;
When that little inner voice said,
You know you can't go!

My thoughts will be with you
As you grace this gala affair!
I would really like to attend,
But alas, I have nothing to wear;
Except this big smile on my face,
And a leaf that just fell in my hair!

Russian Roulette

Our yesterdays
Were bleak and black
And I'm always sad,
When I start to think back!
Like fine china
Our feelings were fragile,
So we put up a front
By wearing a smile!

Rearing children
Is like Russian Roulette!
Lot's of duty and demands,
And many, many regrets!
I deeply desired love and happiness,
But fear this has passed me by,
For with our life
I made a real mess!

Keeping My Distance

Oh, to just be me and bear it all,
But some of my past I can't recall!
It must have really been bad,
'Cause I've nearly always been sad!
I certainly don't like this blockade,
But I do recall times that I was betrayed
With truth about me that I had relayed;
Then I realized why I'm so afraid!
I have one very close friend,
But I haven't really let her in;
There's a fear of taking a chance,
So I just keep my distance!

Thelma, my confidant

Over Sixty-Two

At our class reunion
I drifted back in time,
to our last year in school
when we were in our prime!
Everyone made fun of Ray
for he was skinny as a broom,
now, when he walks across the floor
he shakes the entire room.
Our liveliest cheerleader
once could jump and shout,
but today she can barely walk
because she has the gout!
I didn't even recognize
Tom or Bobbie Sue,
but I must remember
we're over sixty-two!
When I talked to loud mouth Bob
he didn't have much to say,
just put his hand over his mouth
so his dentures wouldn't get away.
I thought my biggest shock
was pretty Betty Lou,
with her pierced tongue and nose
and a shoulder tattoo!

Then I saw Laura Jo,
and I couldn't believe my eyes,
she was once the Good Year Blimp,
Now, "look at those shapely thighs!"
Our physical shape has really changed
except for just a few,
but I think they may have had
a little tuck or two!

Mitzie • Perry • Carlie

Dead On My Feet

Now that you have retired,
At least , it seems that way!
I still have the same old things to do
Day, after day, after day!
I make the beds, sweep, and mop the floors,
Cook and sew, and wash and iron our clothes;
Clean up the yard, and often pause,
To wipe the grandchildren's nose!
I bathe and groom the dogs, burn the trash,
Run errands, and give you personal care;
Pick up your boots, shirt and pants,
And even cut your hair!

So, sometimes if you get hungry,
PLEASE, fix yourself a bite to eat,
For often our appetites aren't the same,
Or I'm just dead on my feet!

When you buy a new car or truck,
You really drive it hard,
When it's older, you go somewhat slower,
And leave it parked more often in the yard!
Well Darling, that's kinda how I feel,
This body is wearing down,
And I need to slow my pace,
Or I may no longer be around!
So, "I ask you," please remember,
When "you ask me" to bring you this or that,
Like YOU, I am only human and have feelings too;
NOT, just someone to fetch, or pick up your hat!

Gracie, my great granddaughter

Kalee, my great granddaughter

Mackenzie, my great granddaughter

The Lonely Guitar

The Guitar stands silent, in the light of the moon,
awaiting the master's hand, to pick out a new tune!
The body of the master is still somewhere around,
but the mind and soul can no longer be found!
His mind sees a lonely sea, with no way to navigate,
or perhaps he's asking God, why he feels so desolate!
The Guitar says, "Come back! Our songs aren't that bad,
some of them are uplifting, but you're always so sad!
You try too hard to please and just leave me
alone to grieve!
You forget about my feelings, but I know what
we can achieve!
Come on, touch me gently, just like you used to do,
I know you're feeling low, but I still love you.
HEY! Look at me, come on glance my way!
I'm begging you, p l e a s e, pick me up, let's play.
We might get a new sound that would
make you smile.
I'll surely make you happy, for just a little while!
I know about your troubles, that you're
lonely and blue,
but I'm all alone in this corner, and I'm
lonely for you!
Come on! Pick me up, sing me a lullaby!
If you don't feel better, we'll both cry!"

Randi, my great granddaughter

Heartache—One-Two

I was only seventeen; my heart was in full bloom,
you were like a gentle breeze, on a summer afternoon.
I knew it was wrong, when I shared your bed,
but I listened to my heart, and ignored my head.

Jesus was first, now it's money, booze, and fame,
I'm just a stepping stone, as you play life's game.
My heart keeps saying, please listen to your head
he's only using you, just to warm up his bed.

So now I'm moving on, oh how my heart aches,
I wish this was a dream, from which I could awake.
I'm not asking for much, I hope you understand,
only loyalty and love, sacred vows, a wedding band!
Heartache—one-two!

Star Dodger

Just as the dawn was breaking,
a new colt lay wet on the hay.

Then, long legs still shaking,
he stood by his mama, the Gray.

A reddish tan and a white blaze face,
with eyes so gentle and kind;

Star held his head with poise and grace,
and captured this heart of mine!

Gray turned on him; whenever he got close
she would kick and bite.

He only wanted to be loved and nurse,
oh, such a sad, sad sight!

Star soon came to depend,
on bottle milk and T L C;

And the soothing voice of a friend,
that couldn't see his destiny.

Just a tender touch or pat on the back,
he would play in the melting snow.

A halter and rope and a little slack,
he ran like the wind or pranced like a pro.

Alone in his stall so bleak and black,
he would call with a whinny and neigh;

But his legs were getting very weak,
when he stood on his bed of hay.

Kicked and bitten from the very start,
he tried to dodge her every move.

His mama's rejection broke his heart,
and Star lost his will to improve!

Corky

Our Loss

A husband, a dad, a friend,
they say in time, our hurt will mend.
You were truly one of a kind,
a better friend, no one could find.
You were always helping others,
be it kin, friend, sisters, or brothers!
Plenty of folks looked up to you,
but nary a one, can fill your shoe!
You had your opinion on everything,
from the price of land, to a diamond ring!
Nothing will ever take your place
we hold dear, your handsome face!
There are no words, that we can say,
of how we feel, on this sad, sad day!
Your life and breath has ceased to be,
but memories of you will last for an eternity!

Carl C. "Bill" Thrasher

Those Salty Tears

Today I'm lonely and blue,
another year has come and gone,
and I've not seen any of you.
Every now and then I see a familiar face,
we sometimes stop and chat,
but my old time friends, they just can't replace.

Oh, such sweet memories rush past my mind's eye,
and my heart aches when I think of past years,
then I begin to cry.
I really cherish the times we all had back then,
and sometimes even wish,
to relive it once again!

If ever again,
I feel your warm embrace
I know my heart will leap with joy
as Christ wipes away the taste,
of those salty tears,
that often stain my face!

Carlie

The Tangled Web

Oh what a tangled web I weave,
when I allow my mind to roam.
For I often find myself, anywhere but home.
Life is like a mountain,
that I've been told to climb.
Seems I'm caught in winter,
with no springtime.
Should I follow my dream,
or give up and stay?
Oh Lord my God,
please help me to know the way.
My heart cries,
"Look," I have a lot of love to give.
But then, I hear a voice say, NO,
you don't even have a reason to live!
Life on earth is cruel, must I shout?
You don't have the strength to stay,
take the easy way out.
Easy, I ask, but what about the broken hearts
I'd leave behind,
aren't they more important than mine?
"Think of a high spirited horse,
brought in off the range,
she fights to the end with fury and rage.
But finally with spirit broken,
she's trapped like a bird in a cage!

Now she obeys every command,
never again to be free!
She no longer stands proud,
only bent low, with her head tied to a tree.
Oh what a shame, Oh what a shame,
no more will she roam to and fro:
What a tangled web I weave,
regardless of which way I go!"
Someone will grieve,
should I stay or should I leave,
should it be them, or should it be me?
I don't know! I don't know!

Carlie

Hiding Behind Laughter

Behind this laughter, young, full of life
happy and carefree; twinkles in the eyes,
ever smiling: hiding behind this laughter is me!

To give to others so they are happy
for them I do smile, cheerful for all to see;
but laughter is a disguise, for the secrets I keep,
the eternal tears I weep!

Sometimes I remember those that said
they'd always care,
then I search for a true friend,
yet not find one anywhere!

I seldom ask for anything,
and give as much as I dare!
Everyone needs to be loved,
with special feelings to share!

But time goes on—I accept,
this I will not receive;
far too many have carelessly cast aside
something that was very special to me!

Somewhere in my heart lives a happy song,
waiting for it's turn, but tears drown it out
and the laughter that burns.

Is reality, life, a forever changing tune?
Or is it laughter and tears,
the need for someone to care?
The answer I fear!

Terry, my son

Self-Pity

**Cast me not away from thy presence; and take not
thy holy spirit from me. Restore unto me the joy of
thy salvation; and uphold me with thy free spirit.**

—PSALMS 51:11–12

Too many times this path I trod,
For I had lost the sight of God!
I felt self-pity, a lot of shame,
And my tears flowed like rain.
The wrong way I tried to escape,
And I'm still paying for that mistake!
Once, death looked better than my misery,
But the face of my love ones appeared to me!
Then a voice said, "Hold on, don't let Satan win!"
Deliverance came, when I let Christ back in!

Life Is a Journey

**But they that wait upon the Lord
shall renew their strength.**

—ISAIAH 40; 30 A

I can take most irritations
With a grain of salt,
'Cause for me,
Christ died,
And Him I will exult!
He's prepared for me
A better place,
I rise early,
Smell the coffee,
And wait!
Life,
Is a precious journey
And this I appreciate!

Troubled, Uptight Mind

For I acknowledge my transgressions:
and my sin is ever before me.
Against thee, thee only, have I sinned,
and done this evil in thy sight.

—PSALMS 51: 3–4 A

My sins are ever present
And evil I do see.
Dear God, please erase,
This vision from me!
I'm so tired of mental pain,
Let my conscious be at rest,
I know I'll never be perfect,
But I offer you my best!
Fill my heart with laughter,
Just allow me to unwind,
Oh Lord, please release,
My troubled, uptight mind!

The Mind That Binds

For by grace are ye saved through faith; and that not of yourselves: it is the gift of God. Not of works, lest any man should boast.

—EPHESIANS 2:8–9

I struggle to change
The mind that binds me!
And seek, what could be!
But legalism,
Is embedded deep within
And my mind is my enemy!
It clings to the rules I broke,
And, hasty words I spoke!
Christ hung on the cross,
And died in agony,
To abolish those laws,
And set us free!
Old habits are hard to break,
And no truer words, ere' I spake!

Trust Jesus

He that believeth on him is not condemned:
but he that believeth not is condemned already,
because he hath not believed in the name
of the only begotten Son of God.

—JOHN 3:18

I'm joint-heir with the King,
And God, my Father, owns everything!

Do you have sweet fellowship with Him?
Or does eternity look really grim?

Will you trust Jesus as Savior and Lord?
And live in heaven in sweet accord?

Heaven or hell; where will it be?
Where will your soul spend eternity?

Please, please repent of your sin,
Don't leave this world forever condemned!

My Heart Cried

*Be sober, be vigilant; because your adversary
the devil, as a roaring lion, walketh about,
seeking whom he may devour.*

—1 PETER 5:8

When
my heart cried
God was listening,
to how I felt inside!
Now I can laugh and sing,
thank you God, for Christ the King!
My problems no longer seem so bad,
with Jesus beside me I don't feel so sad!
He was always there I just could not see,
because the lies of the devil had blinded me!
If only my love ones would just trust in You,
in heaven we could all have a happy rendezvous.

The Woman-Child

But Jesus said, Suffer little children,
and forbid them not,
to come unto me: for of such is
the kingdom of heaven.

—ST. MATTHEW 19:14

Looking over a mountain steep,
into the valley deep,
I saw a girl, "little misfit,"
left alone in a miry pit!
Beaten down by family and foe,
all because she was "slow"!
A woman outside, a child within,
only desiring a true friend!
Oh, how she needs You, Dear God,
to guide her on this earth we trod!
Even when she's feeling blue,
twinkling eyes come beaming thru.
Her spirit speaks to mine,
with a smile, like warm sunshine!
Her child like mind is easy to sway!
dear Lord, have mercy, I do pray!

My Father Loves Me

**Blessed is the man that trusteth in the Lord,
and whose hope the Lord is.**

—JEREMIAH 17:7

Today it's windy and cold,
and the rain is falling,
but I can feel the Son!
I know my Father loves me
and by His Spirit I am led,
though sometimes I feel undone!
Praise God for His blessings,
He knows what is ahead,
and provides strength to overcome!

Stacie, my granddaughter

Satan's Charm

But every man is tempted, when he is drawn
away of his own lust, and enticed.
—JAMES 1:14

At times my load is hard to carry.
God wants me closer to him,
but with Satan's charm I tarry.
Lust is Satan's tool,
at times I'm spiritually blind!
All too often I become the fool;
through my eyes and mind!
I arise lifted up, from lip of others
I'm often torn down,
I'd like to have a beautiful smile,
but Satan had rather that I frown!
He likes to inflict torment,
I try to avoid him like a plague,
but sometimes I feel as though
I'm sitting on a powder keg!

Tracie, my granddaughter

Praise God

The LORD is my rock, and my fortress, and my deliverer; my God, my strength, in whom I will trust.
—PSALMS 18:2 A

I tell myself it's forgotten,
That I don't hurt anymore;
But tucked away in a dark corner,
I've never really closed the door!

At the first sign of weakness,
Satan pounces like a lion;
Reminding me of past heartaches,
But Jesus intercedes, each time!

The mercy of Jesus is like a rose
That smells so fresh and sweet;
For me, death on the cross He chose;
His resurrection made it complete!

I'm slowly learning to forgive,
And to exemplify Him I count as joy!
Jesus dwells within where'er I live,
Yet my temple Satan tries to destroy!

*San Juan
Mountain*

A Mother's Prayer

Neither is there salvation in any other:
for there is none other name under heaven given
among men, whereby we must be saved.
—ACTS 4:12

A mother was praying for her son that day like many
times before; she was down on her knees pleading,
Lord please; draw him into Your fold.

Oh Lord, Dear Lord, he wanders in darkness, like raging
wildfires he's filled with bitterness and rage; for Satan has
stolen his mind with drugs and evil desires.

It was so quiet she could hear her heart-beat and each
tear that fell to the floor; but the silence was broken
by heavy footsteps, as he stormed out the door.

Dear God, You sacrificed Your precious Son when He
gave His life for me; Oh Lord, I'll trade my life to see
my son set free and know that his soul belongs to Thee!

Then, with me the angels will shout and sing praise
to our King; for he was lost and wandered in sin,
but now is found and standing on solid ground!
AMEN

Believe

Those by the way side are they that hear; then
cometh the devil, and taketh away the word out of
their hearts, lest they should believe and be saved.

—ST. LUKE 8:12

I Am the great I AM!
I gave My Son for you,
I Am the one
That loves you true!
I Am the great I Am!
God's word they heard
But where did it go:
Satan just whisked it away,
And they didn't even know!
Eternal separation from God
Is more than my heart can bare,
But a lot of my love ones,
Don't even seem to care!

My Goal

*Trust in the LORD with all thine heart; and lean
not unto thine own understanding. In all thy ways
acknowledge him, and he shall direct thy paths.*

—PROVERBS 3:5–6

I want to walk, not run,
Take time to listen,
To the Father and his
Only begotten Son!
I'm forging on,
Thru high and low;
While keeping
My sight on Christ,
While I journey
In this earth below!
I look but do not see,
What it is I should be!
My past you know,
My future too;
So I await
To hear from You!

Christmas—
A Gift of Love

And God said, Let us make man in our image,
after our likeness.

—GENESIS 1:26 A

I was thinking back in time,
when everything was perfect
and there was no crime.
God had a master plan and said,
in our image let us make man.
Us, means more than one,
there was God the Father,
and God the Son!
In heaven above,
Jesus was with God,
where everything was love!
Man was made from dust,
given the breath of life,
with love faith and trust!
But man forgot to pray;
then Satan stepped in,
and man was led astray!

To fulfill the Fathers plan
a virgin gave birth,
thus, Jesus became a man.
The gift of love was given
through Jesus Christ
when He came from heaven!
Let us praise the King
God is love,
hallelujah, shout and sing!
We don't need a video game
tinsel, trees, and lights,
or fortune and fame!
So if your wallet looks bare
give the gift of love
and show someone you care!
Love we will remember;
not just at Christmas time,
but from January thru December!

An Old-Fashion Christmas

Let's have an old-fashion Christmas,
like they had long ago!
When they cut a tree in the woods,
and played in glistening snow!
We'll string holly-berries,
hang up the mistletoe,
say our prayers to Jesus,
then off to bed we'll go!

Jesus Lord, and Savior,
we celebrate your birth,
with gifts of love, from one another,
and a tree from your green earth!

We'll cook the old red rooster,
fruit cake, and pumpkin pie!
See the falling snow on the window,
and watch the redbirds fly!
We'll make taffy candy,
and colored popcorn balls,
bow our head in prayer,
and thank Jesus for it all!

'Tis the Day After

For ye are bought with a price: therefore glorify God in your body, and in your spirit, which are God's.
—1 CORINTHIANS 6:20

'Tis the day after Christmas and down the dark hall,
all is so quiet I can hear the leaves fall!
Wrapping paper and boxes strewn over the floor,
and the shopping and baking is finally o'er!
My family and friends have all gone home,
and once again I'm here all alone!
I'm really exhausted, I do confess,
and now I must clean up this awful mess!
As I busy myself with the household tasks,
in my mind these questions I ask!
Was all the hustle and bustle wisely spent;
and how much time was heavenly sent?
Was our family and church in one accord;
and did we bring joy to our Lord?
Did we show love to one and all,
or does our heart need and overhaul?
Was Jesus birth glorified;
or did He somehow get pushed aside?
This year is coming to and end
and a New Year is just around the bend!
Oh Lord! You know our hearts, each one;
may we truly exalt, Your precious Son!

Satan will try to manipulate,
Trust Jesus . . .
and don't wait too late!

About the Author

Carlie Thrasher Downey

I'm a born and country-bred East Texan. Though I grew up with meager means, my loving parents made sure I had everything I needed. However, they balked at my wheedling to get "things" just because my friends had new clothes and gadgets. Mother taught me domestic skills such as sewing, cooking, gardening, and ironing (ugh!), and keeping a very clean house; and Dad taught me fishing, camping, hunting, and such, which we thoroughly enoyed as a family (with the exception of my sister, for she was such a little lady that dirt disgusted her to no end!). As a family, we also played the games 42 and Dominos.

At a very young age I discovered talking in rhyme, so much so that I used this gift to irritate my motherly sister. As a child I had no brothers to play with, so when I was thirteen I discovered BOYS! I was married at the tender age of sixteen, became the mother of a beautiful daughter at eighteen, and as time passed we also had two handsome sons. Our family has also been blessed with two loving granddaughters and four great-granddaughters!

I didn't know Jesus as my Lord and Savior until I was almost thirty. He is the Light in my life and many times He has allowed me to witness to and council with some very hurting people. As a form of release for me, I would write poems about their sad lives—sometimes using objects or animals so as not to use their names!

Our children's dad, (E.J. McGee) died in 2001 at the young age of 65. In 2005 I married my hero, Cecil, a true servant of God and a World War II survivor of Iwo Jima. Cecil lost both legs at the age of 20 and lived 63 more years with the use of a wheelchair. Sadly we only had two and a half wonderful years before the Lord called him to his heavenly home!

Currently, I use my musical gifts of singing and playing a 12-string guitar to entertain in and around our area.

9780985372590